BLURT BEANS

Jennifer Jones

BLURT BEANS

Jennifer Jones

This is a story about Blurt Beans,
Do you know what those are?
When you blurt something out,
You have to put beans inside a Blurt Jar!

A blurt happens when you talk,
Without getting permission to speak.
It's a silly word for when you can't help it,
But out your words sneak!

Sometimes it's so hard,
To hold your thoughts in and not share,
So you say what's in your head,
Without a second care.

Well, apparently our class
Was extra talkative one day, you see.
Everyone was speaking out of turn,
Especially — you guessed it—ME!

Our teacher was frustrated,
And didn't know what to say.
She promised there'd be NO MORE BLURTING,
When she came to class the next day.

"But how?" we wondered.
"We're not doing it on purpose, you know?"
"Yes!" our teacher answered.
"I must find a solution, though!"

The next morning, we arrived
To find small jars on our desks.
The jars were empty,
And held no material or objects.

Next to each jar,
There were five little beans.
We looked at each other and asked,
"What does this mean?"

"Good morning, students," she said,
Greeting us as we walked in.
"I'll explain the beans,
And what the jars will hold within."

These are Blurt Beans.
They will help us stop blurting out.
She held one of the jars up,
And told us what this game was all about.

"Each time you speak without raising your hand,
You'll put a bean in your jar.
I'm confident you'll be surprised
At how disciplined you all are!"

The beans that stayed outside the jars,
For when we didn't blurt,
Would go into a big class jar,
And do you know what they would be worth?

Cool rewards, more free time,
And even a pajama day!
The Class jar would collect the beans
For the blurts we did NOT say!

MOVIE POPCORN PARTY

PAJAMA PARTY

FREE TIME

COOL REWARDS

The first day with our jars,
Most of us had to put in a few blurt beans.
But the longer we had our jars,
Less blurting out was easier than it seemed.

MOVIE POPCORN PARTY

PAJAMA PARTY

FREE TIME

COOL REWARDS

We got used to raising our hands,
And soon, the classroom jar was full.
We got a movie popcorn party,
Which was really, really cool!

So if you find yourself talking a lot,
Without raising your hands too,
Maybe you can talk to your teacher
About making a blurt jar for you!

Printed in the USA
CPSIA information can be obtained
at www.ICGtesting.com
LVHW061643281223
767654LV00017B/125